FIRST REPERTOIRE FOR
CLARINET

with piano

edited, selected and arranged by
ausgewählt, herausgegeben und bearbeitet von
choisi, édité et arrangé par

Paul Harris
&
Emma Johnson

© 2003 by Faber Music Ltd
First published in 2003 by Faber Music Ltd
3 Queen Square London WC1N 3AU
Cover illustration by Drew Hillier
Cover design by Nick Flower
Music processed by Jackie Leigh
Printed in England by Caligraving Ltd

ISBN 0-571-52165-7

To buy Faber Music publications or to find out about the full range of titles available
please contact your local music retailer or Faber Music sales enquiries:

Faber Music Limited, Burnt Mill, Elizabeth Way, Harlow, CM20 2HX England
Tel: +44 (0)1279 82 89 82   Fax: +44 (0)1279 82 89 83
sales@fabermusic.com   fabermusic.com

CONTENTS

Rigadoon for the mock trumpet

Anonymous

This piece comes from the very first method for the clarinet written in 1706.
Because of its rather raucous sound the early clarinet was often called the 'mock trumpet'!

Theme from *Inspector Morse*

Barrington Pheloung

repeat to fade

Contredanse en rondeau

from Divertimento No.8 K.213

Wolfgang Amadeus Mozart
(1756–1791)

Hagley's tune

Hagley West

8ve ad lib.

The penguins take a stroll

Paul Harris

Coventry carol

16th-century English carol

A groovy kind of sonatina

based on a Sonatina by Clementi

arr. PH/EJ
Muzio Clementi
(1752–1832)

Prélude

Charles-Valentin Alkan
(1813–1888)

Potpourri

from Concertpiece No.3 for clarinet and string quartet

Franz Danzi
(1763–1826)

FIRST REPERTOIRE FOR
CLARINET

clarinet part

edited, selected and arranged by
ausgewählt, herausgegeben und bearbeitet von
choisi, édité et arrangé par

Paul Harris
&
Emma Johnson

© 2003 by Faber Music Ltd
First published in 2003 by Faber Music Ltd
3 Queen Square London WC1N 3AU
Cover illustration by Drew Hillier
Cover design by Nick Flower
Music processed by Jackie Leigh
Printed in England by Caligraving Ltd
All rights reserved
ISBN 0-571-52165-7

CONTENTS

Rigadoon for the mock trumpet

Anonymous

This piece comes from the very first method for the clarinet written in 1706.
Because of its rather raucous sound the early clarinet was often called the 'mock trumpet'!

4

Theme from *Inspector Morse*

Barrington Pheloung

Contredanse en rondeau

from Divertimento No.8 K.213

Wolfgang Amadeus Mozart
(1756–1791)

6

Hagley's tune

Brightly (♩ = c.126)

The penguins take a stroll

Paul Harris

Con moto (♩ = c.132)

Coventry carol

16th-century English carol

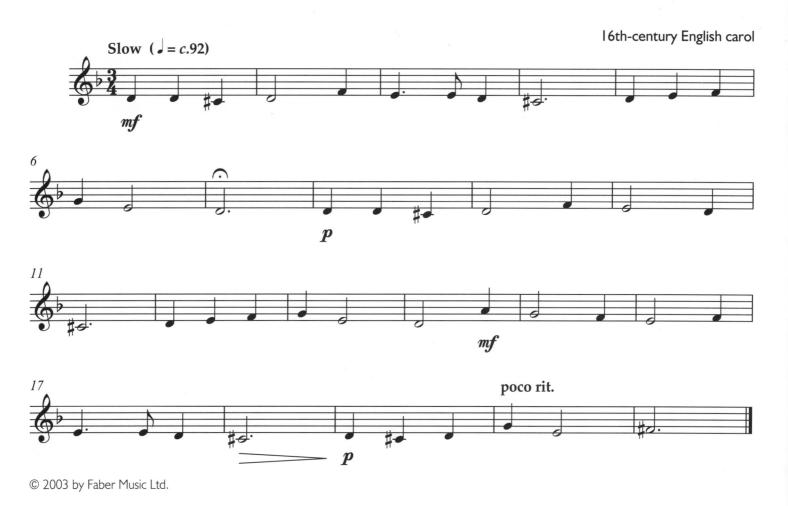

A groovy kind of sonatina
based on a Sonatina by Clementi

arr. PH/EJ
Muzio Clementi
(1752–1832)

Prélude

Charles-Valentin Alkan
(1813–1888)

Potpourri

from Concertpiece No.3 for clarinet and string quartet

Franz Danzi
(1763–1826)

The spy who went out to the cold

Paul Harris

Witches' dance

Theodor Kullak
(1818–1882)

Night and day

Cole Porter
(1891–1964)

* Use the side B♭ fingering.

Burlesque

from Sonatina Romantica

Benjamin Britten
(1913–1976)

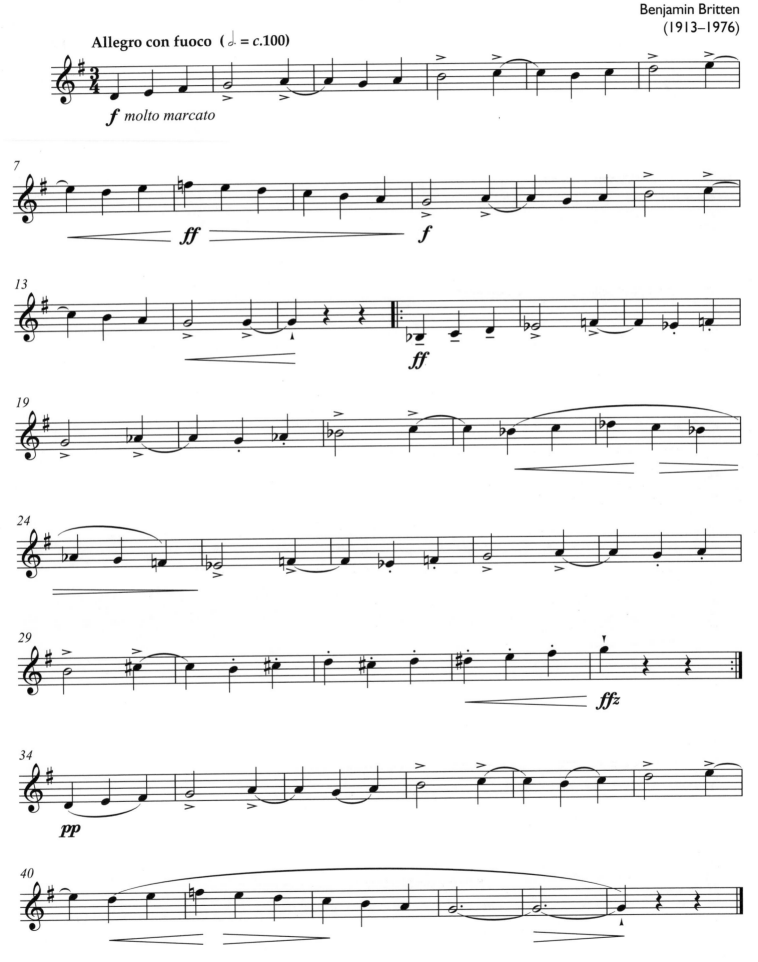

Vivace
3rd movement *from* Concerto for 2 clarinets

Georg Philipp Telemann
(1681–1767)

Swedish dance

Max Bruch
(1838–1920)

Georgie

Emma Johnson

poco rit.

The spy who went out to the cold

Paul Harris

Witches' dance

Theodor Kullak
(1818–1882)

Allegro animato (♩ = c.160)

Night and day

Cole Porter
(1891–1964)

Moderato (♩ = c.120)

* Use the side B♭ fingering.

Burlesque

from Sonatina Romantica

Benjamin Britten
(1913–1976)

Vivace

3rd movement *from* Concerto for 2 clarinets

Georg Philipp Telemann
(1681–1767)

Swedish dance

Max Bruch
(1838–1920)

Georgie

Emma Johnson

poco accel.   poco rit.   a tempo

rit.

CUTTING-EDGE MUSIC WITH COOL CD BACKING

Groove Lab contains ten pieces reflecting current sounds and styles, including Techno, House, Garage and Ambient.

Professional backing tracks encourage confident performance every time

Each piece includes a second, extended version for experimentation and improvisation

Suitable for performers at Grades 2–4

Groove Lab is co-written by Andy Hampton and David Motion

FABER *ff* MUSIC